We Are All Different

Jayden Coll-Seck

Rosen REAL READERS

Rosen Classroom™
New York

My friends are all different.

We come from different places.

We look different.

We wear different clothes.

We like different things.

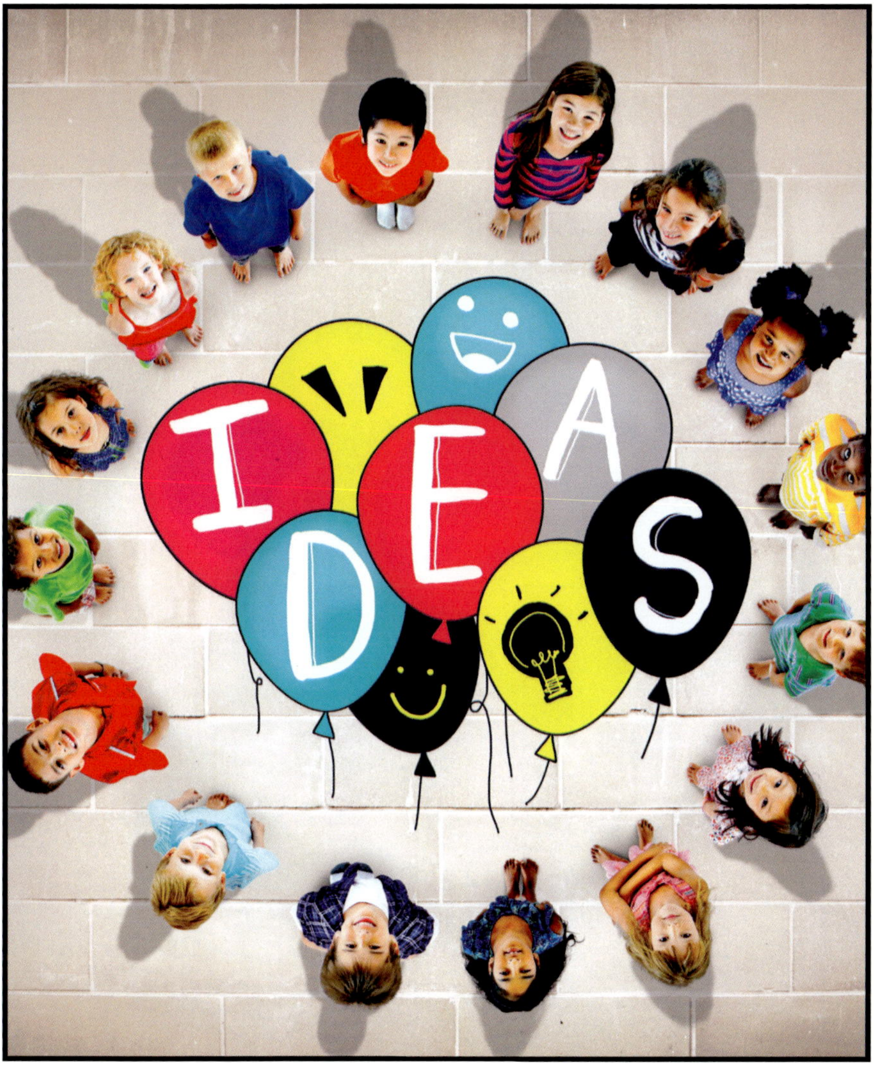

We have different ideas.

Words To Know

clothes

friends

ideas

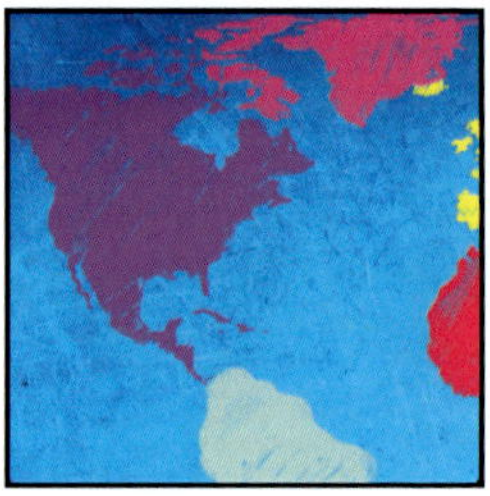

places